Guess where I live

illustrated by Anni Axworthy

WALKER BOOKS
AND SUBSIDIARIES
LONDON · BOSTON · SYDNEY

D0349590

Where do I live?

This is me.
I'm a monkey.

My home is hot and there are lots of trees.

It rains nearly every day.

Snakes and parrots live here, too.

Jungles are also
called rainforests.

Where do I live?

This is me. I'm a Polar bear.

My home is cold and snowy.

And there are lots of icebergs.

Seals and foxes live here, too.

The Arctic is the icy land around the North Pole.

Where do I live?

This is me.
I'm a crab.

There are
lots of rocks
and seaweed.

y home is
der water.

Starfish and limpets
live here, too.

Lots of small sea animals live in the shallow water by the coast.

Where do I live?

This is me.
I'm a camel.

My home is very hot and dry.

There are lots of sandy hills.

Lizards and scorpions live here, too.

Deserts are places where it hardly ever rains.

Where do I live?

This is me. I'm a Golden eagle.

My home is rocky and high up.

And sometimes it snows a lot.

Goats and hares live here, too.

On the top of high mountains the snow never melts.

We're in the wrong homes! Can you remember where we really live?

First published 1999 by Walker Books Ltd
87 Vauxhall Walk, London SE11 5HJ

2 4 6 8 10 9 7 5 3 1

Series concept and design by Louise Jackson

Words by Louise Jackson and Paul Harrison

Wildlife consultant: Martin Jenkins

Text © 1999 Walker Books Ltd
Illustrations © 1999 Anni Axworthy

This book has been typeset in Joe Overweight.

Printed in Singapore

British Library Cataloguing in Publication Data
A catalogue record for this book is available
from the British Library.

ISBN 0-7445-6230-9